AF574660
LONDON MIDLAND
STEAM ON SHED
MORE GREAT WESTERN STEAM IN DEVON
SOUTHERN STEAM IN ACTION
AROUND THE WORLD
BORDERS STEAM
LIGHT RAILWAYS
standard gauge and narrow gauge
OF BRITAIN
ARTICULATED LOCOMOTIVES OF THE WORLD
MAIN LINE STEAM
STEAM IN india
GREAT WESTERN STEAM THROUGH THE YEARS
SCOTTISH RAILWAYS in the heyday of steam
WESTERNS
THE WELSH NARROW GAUGE
SUPERPOWER STEAM
BRITISH TRAMS
SCOTTISH
BRANCH LINE STEAM
THE MIDLAND RAILWAY
AROUND THE WORLD
the later years of
LMSR LOCOMOTIVES
GREAT WESTERN

WELSH RAILWAYS
in the heyday of steam

75016

WELSH RAILWAYS

in the heyday of steam

H. C. CASSERLEY

D. BRADFORD BARTON LTD

Frontispiece: an impressive view, taken on 28 August 1966, of the 6.05 p.m. Aberystwyth-Shrewsbury ('The Mail') near Talerddig Summit, on the former Cambrian main line. [M. Mensing]

IRRC 7801/3BL *ISBN 0 85153 357 4*

printed in Great Britain by H. E. Warne Ltd, London and St. Austell

for the publishers

D. BRADFORD BARTON LTD · Trethellan House · Truro · Cornwall · England

introduction

Following the general pattern of the two previous volumes in this series, embracing Ireland and Scotland, the period covered herein has been based largely on the years between the wars plus the final decade of the 1950s and 1960s, when steam was rapidly being ousted by the diesel. The beginnings of the preservation era are not overlooked; it would have been inappropriate, in Wales of all countries, entirely to ignore the very beginnings of this movement, which started with the Talyllyn and now embraces the 'Great Little Trains of Wales', even if their mention is necessarily brief. At the other end of the scale, there are for good measure a few incursions into the pre-1914 era.

The selection of the illustrations, a good many from the author's own camera, as well as from a wide range of other sources, is chosen to provide as much variety as possible; trains in motion from all angles, in scenic surroundings, with necessarily a fair number of static views of the locomotives of the numerous independent railways in South Wales absorbed by the G.W.R. at the grouping. Of these latter at work very few satisfactory photographs are available or even known to exist. A large proportion of the main line classes which have worked on the lines of the Principality from the 1930s onwards will be found to be represented and with surprisingly few duplications, except inevitably for the ubiquitous G.W.R. pannier tanks, resulting in a book with a more than usually wide variety of subjects.

H. C. Casserley

A view near Penmaenmawr about 1920 of an up Holyhead express headed by 'Renown' rebuilc No.1968 *Cumberland* piloting an unidentified 'Prince of Wales' 4-6-0.

The North Wales coast line of the former Chester & Holyhead Railway (later L.N.W.R. and L.M.S.); the up 'Welshman' leaving Colwyn Bay about 1930 with 'Claughton' No.5968 *John O' Groat* (built 1920 and scrapped 1935).

A scene on the North Wales coast line in later years; the 4.15 p.m. Manchester–Llandudno train leaving Rhyl on 23 August 1959 behind Stanier 'Black Five' No.44910. [M. Mensing]

PLATFORM
3
COLWYN
NEXT TRAIN
WILL DEPART AT
THE LINE
BRIDGE
OUT

Colwyn Bay about 1910, well depicted by the fashions of the period; an up express for Rhyl, Chester and Liverpool headed by an unidentified Whale 4–4–0 'Precursor'.

In the height of the holiday season trains came to Llandudno from far and wide, even worked through by 'foreign' locomotives, such as this North Stafford 2-4-0 — N.54, built at Stoke in 1906. Seen here on a train for Derby, 19 July 1909.

L.N.W.R. Webb 2-4-2T No.6666 at Llandudno Junction, 3 June 1932.

L.N.W.R. Webb 'Cauliflower' 0-6-0 No.8392 at Bettws-y-Coed, 3 June 1932.

A wartime photograph of 'Royal Scot' No.6133 *The Green Howards* with 'The Irish Mail' passing Llanfairfechan, 17 July 1941. Photography was a risky business in those days, with constant threat of arrest. This one, like a number of others, was taken from the security of a hotel bedroom window.

A local train for Holyhead at Menai Bridge, 12 August 1953, with compound No. 41108. This station was closed to passenger traffic in February 1966.

The famous Britannia Bridge over the Menai Straits; linking Anglesey with the mainland, and completed by Robert Stephenson in 1850. A local train with Webb 0-6-2T No. 7629 is seen in this view taken during the 1930s. The structure has been considerably rebuilt since a disastrous fire in May 1970.

One of the two branches off the main line in Anglesey ran to Amlwch, on the north coast of the island; this is the branch train with L.M.S. type 2-6-2T No. 41233 on 12 August 1953. The branch was entirely closed in December 1964. [R. M. Casserley]

A train from Manchester approaching Holyhead on 14 August 1965 behind B.R. 4-6-0 No. 73053. [R. J. Buckley]

The pleasant setting of Bangor station and shed, 25 June 1956. A Caernarvon train is at the platfor with 2-6-4T No.42417 whilst in the siding is former L.&Y.R. 0-6-0 No.52230.

The branch from Caernarvon to Llanberis, at the foot of Snowdon, ceased to see regular passeng traffic as long ago as September 1932, but during the holiday season special trains ran until it w entirely closed in September 1964. 2-6-4T No.42444 is seen here with a special on 14 August 195 Snowdon can be seen in the background.

An early view of the old Admiralty Pier at Holyhead, with 'The Irish Mail' departing behind an unidentified Webb six-coupled 'Special tank'.

Dinas Junction about 1910. This was situated on the southern extremity of the L.M.S. in the North Wales area, from Caernarvon to Afon Wen (where it made contact with the Cambrian Railways [see page 28]). The train at the platform, headed by an L.N.W.R. 'Cauliflower' 0-6-0, is bound for Afon Wen, whilst on the right is the yard of the North Wales Narrow Gauge Railway (later the Welsh Highland). At the time of writing there are plans to re-open part of the line with the possibility of an extension north over part of the trackbed of the old L.N.W.R. line (closed in 1957), as seen in this illustration.

The L.N.E.R. seems an unlikely candidate for inclusion in a book dealing exclusively with railways in Wales, but it does so by virtue of the former Wrexham Mold & Connah's Quay Railway, which penetrated the county of Flint, within the borders of the Principality. There were considerable deposits of coal in this area. The W.M. & C.Q.R. was taken over by the Great Central in February 1901, and thus eventually became part of the L.N.E.R. system. This view shows a Seacombe-Wrexham train at Hawarden Bridge Halt, adjacent to the Shotton steelworks, on 10 August 1953, headed by former Great Central 4-4-2T No.67412. [R. M. Casserley]

A Dolgellau to Ruabon train entering Llangollen on 31 May 1932 with G.W.R. 2-6-0 No.7308. This route is now completely closed.

Llangollen again, in post-war years, with Collett 0-6-0 No.2297. Although the last trains ran in 1968, a preservation society, initially known as the Flint & Deeside Railway, but now the Llangollen Railway Society, has been formed with a view to re-opening part of the line, possibly as far as Corwen.

Another scene on the now-closed G.W.R. route from Chester to the shores of Cardigan Bay; the 5.40 p.m. Bala-Wrexham is seen skirting the bank of the River Dee just west of Glyndyfrdwy, 5 October 1963, headed by 0-6-0PT No. 4683. [M. Mensing]

4-6-0 No.7827 *Lydham Manor* entering Bala Junction on 15 August 1953 with a Wrexham-Barmouth train.

Bala Junction is one of the half-dozen or so stations in Britain with no public access or booking arrangements; its only function was to provide interchange facilities between main line trains and branch connections. This photograph, taken on the same date as the one above, shows 0-4-2T No.5810 running round its train at the branch platform.

BLAENAU
FFESTINIOG

laenau Ffestiniog G.W.R. station on 15 August 1953 with 0-4-2-T No.5810. This branch was closed 1960-1, except for the retention of the northern portion of the line from Trawsfynydd, used to onvey nuclear 'waste' from a power station via the L.M.S. route from Blaenau Ffestiniog to landudno Junction.

Blaenau Ffestiniog was served by three railways, one being the L.N.W.R. (later L.M.S.) — a line that is still active, with diesel multiple units. This view, in steam days (3 June 1932) shows a train for Llandudno headed by L.N.W.R. 'Cauliflower' 0-6-0 No.8405. Present plans at the time of writing are for a new joint station for B.R. trains and the Ffestiniog, when the latter achieves its ultimate object of re-opening the whole of its line from Portmadoc by 1980 or 1981.

n old view of Blaenau Ffestiniog, where the G.W.R. shared a joint station with the narrow gauge festiniog Railway. At this time, the latter railway nevertheless had its own terminal station in the own, known as Duffws.

The Cambrian was the largest independent railway to be absorbed into the Great Western empire at the grouping. It was in fact one of the smaller of the British railways achieving main line status. With some 250 route miles running mainly through magnificent but sparsely inhabited countryside and serving no large industrial towns, its traffic mainly depended on the holiday resorts on the shores of Cardigan Bay, of which Aberystwyth and Barmouth were the most important. For working such a line, it was natural that the majority of its locomotive stock should have been tender engines, latterly 4-4-0s for passenger work, and 0-6-0s for goods. This view shows a typical example of the 4-4-0s at Oswestry, former headquarters of the Cambrian, but on a section of the line which has now been closed. No. 1082, formerly Cambrian No. 19, was built at the company's own workshops at Oswestry in 1901, the first of only two locomotives constructed there. It was scrapped in 1928, and was photographed on 28 August 1926.

The star train over the Cambrian was the 'Cambrian Coast Express' the only named one on the line. This ran between Paddington and Aberystwyth, with a through portion for Pwllheli, detached at Dove Junction. It is seen here passing Moat Lane on 28 September 1957, behin No.7802 *Bradley Manor*.
[R. J. Buckle

The Pwllheli portion of the 'Cambrian Coast Express' approaching Towyn on 10 September 1958; 2-6-2T No.4575 is in charge.
[R. J. Buckley

The last run of the 'Cambrian Coast Express' came on 4 March 1967, on this date being hauled by B.R. Standard Class 4 4-6-0 No. 75033; this photograph was taken two miles east of Breiddin. So ended the 'Heyday of Steam' on the Cambrian, and passenger service over the line is now almost entirely worked by diesel multiple units. [M. Mensing]

Afon Wen was a somewh
isolated junction, where t
Pwllheli line of the
Cambrian made contact
with the L.M.S. metals
from Caernarvon.
No.9018, one of the
'Dukedogs', which were
reconstructions of the 'D
of Cornwall' Class of 189
and the later 'Bulldogs' —
the boiler of the former ar
the frames of the latter —
seen on a train from Pwllh
leaving for Barmouth,
13 August 1933.

One of the surviving
original 'Dukes', No.9054
Cornubia, at Towyn on
25 August 1948.

W.R. 'Barnum'
uble-framed 2-4-0
o.3207, dating from 1889,
Barmouth on
une 1932. These engines
ere regularly seen in this
ea, but were all scrapped
fore the War.

lore modern motive
ower in the shape of
.M.S.-type class 2-6-0
lo.46520, with the 9.45
m. to Dolgellau, leaving
armouth on 22 July 1964.
[R. J. Buckley]

0-4-2T No. 1434 on a Barmouth–Dolgellau motor train near Barmouth Junction, 26 June 1953.
[R. J. Buckley]

The 1.35 p.m. Dovey Junction to Pwllheli, after having crossed Barmouth Bridge, runs into Barmouth on 7 September 1955. The two locomotives are Nos. 9008 and 4599.
[R. J. Buckley]

Dovey Junction, another 'interchange-only' station (see page 21), with No. 4599 running in with a train from Pwllheli, 25 August 1948. The Aberystwyth line is the platform on the left. It will be noted that the station even boasted a refreshment room in those days. It was normal practice for portions for the Barmouth and Aberystwyth lines to be combined or divided at this point.

'Dukedog' No. 9027 and No. 7819 *Hinton Manor* leaving Machynlleth, 23 August 1948.

Another view of Dovey Junction from the Aberystwyth platform (Barmouth line far left), giving some idea of the complicated shunting movements inevitable in the above-mentioned operation.

78000

Builth Road on 15 September 1949: at the Low Level, ex-G.W.R. Dean 0-6-0 No.2556 on a Brecon-Moat Lane train, whilst at the High Level is 'Black Five' No.45298 on one from Shrewsbury to Swansea. Although there was a siding connection between the two routes, there was never any through passenger running between them. [W. A. Camwell]

From Moat Lane Junction, the Mid-Wales line — not to be confused with the Central Wales line of the L.N.W.R., see pages 39-41 — ran southwards through the heart of the country, amongst magnificent scenery, to Talyllyn Junction, where it joined the Brecon & Merthyr for the final stretch into Brecon. Here, No.78000 stands waiting to depart at Moat Lane on 29 June 1956. This was the B.R. development of the L.M.S. Class 2 2-6-0, to which it was almost identical.

Trains passing at Pantydwr, an intermediate station on the Mid-Wales line, 9 September 1949. One of the surviving Dean goods, No.2484, heads the southbound train.

Builth Road Low Level, 30 May 1936, with the 4.50 p.m. to Builth Wells, headed by G.W.R. 0-4-2T No.4874. This engine was then stationed at the small sub-shed at Builth Wells. Note the M.R. clerestory coach visible on the train at the High Level station — the 2.35 p.m. from Swansea (Victoria). [W. A. Camwell]

Three Cocks Junction, where the Cambrian line from Moat Lane and the Midland line from Hereford converged. This view, taken in September 1951, shows ex-Cambrian 0-6-0 No.896 on a train from Moat Lane to Brecon. [R. M. Casserley]

The part of Three Cocks station seen here was actually Cambrian property, although used only by M.R. trains. A portion of a train on the Mid-Wales line can be seen in the background. Johnson Class 3 0-6-0 No.43600 is about to depart with a Brecon-Hereford train, 9 September 1949. This outpost of the Midland Railway was entirely isolated from its main system, as was the Swansea group of lines (see pages 37 and 38).

Brecon station, although owned by the Brecon & Merthyr Railway, was actually the terminal point of trains of three other railways, the Neath & Brecon, the Cambrian as just described and the Midland. This view, taken on 11 September 1951, shows a Neath & Brecon train from Neath with a 0-6-0PT No.3611, and a Midland train in the right hand bay, plus a Mid-Wales train on the left. The station was closed at the end of 1962 and all three radiating lines are now abandoned.

DOWLAIS TOP
46518

3770

The 47 mile-long main line of the Brecon & Merthyr ran over mountainous country, reaching a summit of 1313′ above sea level at Torpantau, with long gradients as severe as 1 in 38. The 11.15 Newport to Brecon is seen at Dowlais Top on 30 September 1957, behind Class 2 2-6-0 No.46518. [G. Daniels]

The Neath & Brecon had its own terminal station at Neath ((Riverside); pannier tank No.3770 is waiting to depart with the 11.25 a.m. to Brecon, 27 September 1958. [R. J. Buckley]

It was curious that one of the four largest railways in the United Kingdom, the Midland, should have had such close associations with one of the minor lines of South Wales, but purely geographical considerations brought about this state of affairs because, as already stated, the Midland's only access to this part of its system lay over the lines of the Neath & Brecon. M.R. passenger trains in later days consisted of a service between Swansea and Brynamman, a small township in Carmarthen, also served by a G.W.R. branch from Llanelli. The M.R. passenger service had been discontinued in 1950 and the G.W.R. one in 1958, whilst both lines were abandoned in 1964. Two pull-and-push trains on the M.R. line are seen here passing at Clydach on 27 August 1948, with motor-fitted 'Jinties' Nos.7480 and 7481.

In later years, the Midland Swansea line was worked entirely by 0-6-0 tanks of original Johnson design, and their later L.M.S. development, the 'Jinties'. At Swansea Upper Bank shed on 27 June 1938 are two of the later Johnson engines, Nos. 7256 (rebuilt with Belpaire boiler) and No. 7258 in original condition, plus an earlier example, No. 1769, dating from 1890.

The Midland station at Swansea (St. Thomas) was closed in September 1950. Here a train is about to depart for Brynamman, headed by L.M.S. 0-6-0T No. 7481.

Like its great rival the Midland, the L.N.W.R. also succeeded in penetrating South Wales with its own route to Swansea. This ran via Craven Arms, on the Shrewsbury & Hereford, and came to be known as the Central Wales line. Although still open today for passenger services, operated only by diesel railcars, the once-busy freight traffic has now been diverted to other routes, and trains such as this — Class 8F 2-8-0 No. 48665 running through Craven Arms *en route* for Swansea on 10 September 1949 — are no longer to be seen.

A view dating from about 1905 of Llandrindod Wells, with a train headed by a couple of L.N.W.R. Webb 2-4-2Ts. [British Railways]

Knucklas Viaduct on the scenic Central Wales line, with ex-L.N.W.R. 0-8-0 No.8895 on a Craven Arms-Llandovery freight, in the mid-1960s.
[W. A. Camwell]

A Shrewsbury to Swansea train entering at Llandovery on 8 September 1951 with Fowler 2-6-4T No.42390. The next section of this line which the train will traverse was jointly owned by the L.M.S. and G.W.R., known as the Vale of Towy Railway.

Builth Road, High Level, where the Central Wales crossed over the Cambrian Mid-Wales line: No. 42307 is leaving with a train from Swansea to Shrewsbury, 12 July 1956. (See pages 33 and 34 for other views of Builth Road.)

A Shrewsbury-Swansea train photographed at Swansea Bay in July 1955; the locomotive is Stanier 2-6-2T No.40097. [T. J. Edgington]

The Swansea & Mumbles was the oldest public passenger carrying railway, not only in Britain, but in the world. Opened in 1804, as the Oystermouth Railway, it carried passengers from 1807, of course with horse traction. Steam engines were introduced in 1877, and were used until 1929, by which time conventional electric tramcars had taken over, and eventually closure took place in 1960. This view shows 0-4-0ST No. 3, built by Brush in 1907, leaving Brynmill Halt with the 5.10 p.m. Mumbles Pier to Swansea train on 13 May 1919.
[K. A. C. R. Nunn per L. C. G. B.]

Swansea (Victoria), terminus of the L. N. W. R. route to Swansea, on 27 June 1938; Webb 0-6-2T No. 7807 is on station pilot duty. This station was closed 1964-5.

Llanelli station, 27 August 1948; G.W.R. No.4981 *Abberley Hall* heads a semi-fast from Carmarthen to Swansea, whilst 0-6-0PT No.3752 in the branch platform wi a local for Llandeilo.

A motor train from Carmarthen to Swansea entering Kidwelly, 7 July 1947, powered by 0-6-0PT No.6425.

vm Mawr, terminus of
: Burry Port &
vendraeth Valley
ilway, 7 July 1947.
)–0PT No. 1957 stands at
: station platform about to
part with the 3.20 p.m. to
rry Port, whilst sister
gine No. 1967 waits in the
ing to form the following
5 p.m. Passenger services
sed here in 1953.

-6-2T No. 4557 shunting at
rymmych Arms, on the
rmer Whitland &
ardigan Railway,
July 1958. Passenger
rvices were withdrawn in
eptember 1962, and this
ne entirely closed the
llowing May.

Clarbeston Road was the junction for Neyland and Milford Haven; No.5953 *Dunley Hall* is entering with a Fishguard-Swansea train in July 1958. In the bay platform with the Neyland branch train is No.8739.

Tenby on the Pembroke branch, with a Whitland-Pembroke train on the left behind 2-6-2T No.5520, passing an up train from Tenby behind 2-6-2T No.4169, piloting 2-6-0 No.7340.

[R. M. Casserley]

Milford Haven, well known as a naval base and fishing port, has one of the largest natural harbours in Britain, and still has the benefit of a passenger service today, one of the few branches in west Wales to do so. In steam days, pannier tank No.3654 stands at the platform on 7 July 1958 with the 6.30 p.m. to Johnstone, where connection was made with the Neyland branch train, on which services were withdrawn in 1964.

The approach to Fishguard Harbour, 12 May 1953; 0-6-0PT No.5716 shunting vans near Fishguard (Goodwick).
[T. J. Edgington]

Lampeter, junction for the Aberayron branch, on the now closed West Wales route between Carmarthen and Aberystwyth, seen in 1913, with a pull-and-push branch train with 0-4-2T No.559. Lampeter was on the route of a grandiose scheme conceived in 1860 for a 207 mile main line linking Manchester with Milford Haven (page 47). Of this, only the 27 miles between Pencader and Strata Florida ever materialised, this being later incorporated into the Aberystwyth-Carmarthen line.

0-6-0PT No.7444 shunting at Green Grove milk depot on the Aberayron branch, opened o 10 May 1951 — only three days after the permanent cessation of passenger trains over the line — scene taken on 7 July 1958. This part of the branch remained in use until 30 September 1973, when th contract with the Milk Marketing Board terminated.

A Carmarthen train waiting to leave Aberystwyth, 26 August 1948, with Collett 0-6-0 No.222 Passenger services ceased in 1965 on this route and much of it was closed, but a short length nea Carmarthen at the southern end is now being reopened by a preservation society known as the Gwi Railway.

7444

BERYSTWYTH
2223

Pannier tank No.6433 with a local train at Abergavenny Junction, where the G.W.R. Hereford to Newport main line made contact with the L.N.W.R. line to Merthyr; 0-8-0 No.49403 is shunting in the sidings. This was a hilly route skirting the northern extremity of the South Wales coalfield, in the course of which it met up with several of the valley lines leading down to Newport and Cardiff.
[R. M. Casserley]

A pre-grouping photograph of a heavy train at Abergavenny hauled by a couple of Webb's 4′ 3″ 0-6-2Ts (Nos.435 and 1338), sturdy if diminutive engines which performed adequately for many years over this arduous route.

n striking contrast to the mall 0-6-2Ts, the other ngines chiefly employed on he Abergavenny-Merthyr ine were large 0-8-0s and 3eames 0-8-4 tanks, onstructed in 1923. One of he latter, No. 7936, is seen t Abergavenny shed in uly 1938.

t had been L. N. W. R. ractice to allocate a specific ngine to the main ocomotive depots for working Engineers' Department trains. These ad usually been an older 2-4-0 of the 6′ variety, the ngine losing its number nd name in the process. The last 'Engineer South Wales' however was a former Midland Johnson ngine of 1876, allocated to Abergavenny between 1933 nd 1936, after which it returned to ordinary service as L. M. S. No. 20155, and survived until 1950.

Brynmawr was the junction for Blaenavon, which joined up with the G.W.R., over which L.N.W.R. trains used to run through to Newport. At one point, at Waenavon, the line rose to an altitude of 1400′ above sea level, one of the highest in the British Isles. Passenger services ceased in 1941 and the line was entirely closed in 1954. This view, taken on 7 July 1938, shows a Merthyr–Abergavenny train behind ex-L.N.W.R. 'Coal Tank' No.7690.

Nantybwch, junction for the L.N.W.R. valley line to Tredegar and Nine Mile Point, also gave through access over the G.W.R. to Newport. On the right is No.27621, on the 7.30 a.m. Merthyr-Abergavenny, whilst the branch train from Tredegar on the left is composed of a single coach with two engines, Nos.27586 and 7721, 26 April 1948.
[W. A. Camwell]

Rhymney Bridge on 27 April 1948; 0-8-0 No.8921 with a freight, and on the left a G.W.R. Rhymney train from Cardiff with a 0-6-2T No.5678. [W. A. Camwell]

A workmen's train photographed between Sirhowy and Nantybwch on 22 July 1955, headed by 0-8-0 No. 49064.
[W. A. Camwell]

Another of the ex-L.N.W.R. 0-8-0s, No. 49409, on a Tredegar-Barry Island excursion at Pontllanfraith, July 1958.
[T. J. Edgington]

A train from Brecon to Newport on the Brecon & Merthyr at Pontsticill Junction, 11 September 1951, with Collett 0-6-0 No. 2227. This was the junction for Merthyr. Much of the Brecon & Merthyr main line is now closed and abandoned, but there are plans to reopen part of it near Pontsticill, as a narrow gauge system to be known as the Brecon Mountain Railway.

It was not often that a branch line terminated at an unstaffed halt, but Old Ynysbwl was one such rare instance. Such halts, usually with nothing more than a primitive shelter for waiting passengers, came into being in the early years of the century, and rapidly spread in country districts all over the country on most railways, particularly the Great Western. Old Ynysbwl platform was opened by the Taff Vale Railway on 6 November 1905. It was closed on 28 July 1952, this view of a pull-and-push train, with pannier tank No.6411 in charge, having been taken on 11 September 1951.

The South Wales Mineral Railway was one of the smaller independent companies, and was taken over by the G.W.R. in January 1908, together with the Port Talbot. It was henceforth worked by the latter, although both retained their nominal independence until the grouping. Regular passenger services between Cymmer and Glyncorrwg ceased as long ago as 1930, although workmen's trains for the benefit of miners continued. The last of these ran between Glyncorrwg and North Rhondda Halt, serving the adjacent colliery. This was in effect another instance of a branch terminating at a halt, although in this case one which never had a publicly advertised service. 0-6-0PT No.9617 is at North Rhondda Halt, July 1958.

The Pwllyrehebog Incline on the former Taff Vale Railway, with its three-quarter mile gradient of 1 in 13 near Tonypandy in the Rhondda Valley, was cable operated with a stationary engine at the summit. It was unusual in that locomotives also worked on the incline, not as the motive power (which was provided by the stationary engine), but as a source of brake power against the possibility of a run away of the wagons. The Taff Vale had three engines built specially for this duty, 0-6-0Ts with coned boilers, a feature that possibly was the first of its kind — but which of course became common practice on the G.W.R. in later years, and eventually with Stanier on the L.M.S. These pioneers, T.V.R. Nos. 141-143 (later G.W.R. Nos. 792-794, and finally Nos. 193-195), dated from 1884. No. 195 is seen here at work on the incline on 4 May 1951. The branch was entirely closed on 1 July 1951.

With the main valleys in South Wales running roughly from north to sou and most of the railways following the course of these, the few lines which ran from east to west had t do so over large viaducts. One of the most famous w that at Crumlin, where the Pontypool to Neath line crossed the valley and railway from Ebbw Vale t Newport. Crossing this o 27 September 1963 is 0-6-2T No.6627. Sadly, th fine structure is now demolished, despite attempts to have it preserved as a national monument. [W. Potte

Walnut Tree Viaduct, where the Taff Vale lines were bridged by the Barry Railway's extension to join the Brecon & Merthyr at Barry Junction. This train on the ex-Taff Vale is boun for Cardiff, headed by 0-6-2T No.6608. This is o of the only three South Wales valley lines still with passenger services, all worked by d.m.u.s. from Cardiff to Treherbert, Merthyr and Rhymney, although a number of the others are still open for coa traffic. [W. Potte

ain from Bridgend to
engwynfi entering Maesteg,
September 1960, with 2-6-2T
.4121. Passenger services ceased
e in 1960.

Brecon & Merthyr train leaving
w Tredegar in July 1958 behind
w Hawksworth 0-6-0PT
.9482, the final variant of the
g line of inside-cylindered
W.R. pannier tanks. This line
s entirely closed in 1962.

Former Rhymney 0-6-2T No. 41, one of the few classes from the former South Wales lines which lasted into the Nationalisation era, leaving Radyr with a freight train, 5 May 1951.

One of the G.W.R. 2-8-0Ts a type widely used in the South Wales coalfields, although they were also to be seen elsewhere on the system, passing Cardiff (Canton) on 24 June 1956.
[R. J. Buckley

A scene at Pyle of a Porthcawl–Tondu train on 13 September 1952. The engine is No. 4405, one of a small class of only eleven introduced in 1904, with 4′ 1½″ driving wheels, for use on branches with severe gradients. [R. J. Buckley]

Former Taff Vale 0-6-2T No. 389, rebuilt with Swindon boiler, on a train entering Barry Island on 5 May 1951. Barry Island is still a popular resort, with a frequent train service from the valley lines of the T.V.R., Barry and Rhymney, (although now of course operated by the inevitable d.m.u.s), particularly at weekends during the summer season.

No.2902 *Lady of the Lake* departing from Cardiff (General) for Swansea, 27 June 1938

Three generations of G.W.R. locomotives were mainly responsible in steam days for expresses between Paddington, Cardiff and Swansea. William Dean's 'Badminton' Class 4-4-0s, when introduced in 1897, superseded 2-4-0s on these South Wales services. The later Churchward developments, the 'Atbara', 'Flower' and 'City' Classes, were very similar, and likewise worked to Swansea and Fishguard until their place was taken by the various 4-6-0 classes, the two-cylinder 'Saints' and four-cylinder 'Stars' and 'Castles', which reigned supreme until the diesel age. One of the original 'Badmintons', No.4116 *Savernake,* photographed at Cardiff (Canton) shed, 1 May 1927.

No.5049 *Denbigh Castle* leaving Newport with a London express on 6 July 1947. In 1950, twenty of these locomotives were allocated to Cardiff, sixteen to Landore (Swansea), while Carmarthen had one. The world-famous 'Kings' were seldom or never seen on the Welsh side of the Severn Tunnel.

The G.W.R. was quick to 'Swindonise' many of its acquisitions, including some of the more unusual oddments, such as this Barry 0-6-2T, No.194, one of five American-built engines of 1899. Even so, its life was short, and it was scrapped in 1930. Barry, 1 May 1927.

Six 0-8-2Ts built in 1896 for the Barry were the first of their type in the United Kingdom. These were never rebuilt and, again, all had gone by 1930; No.1382 at Barry, 1 May 1927.

In the following pages are representative examples of the smaller railways of South Wales, fourteen in all, which were absorbed into the Great Western at the grouping. The miscellaneous and most varied collection of locomotives which the G.W.R. acquired, most of them destined for early extinction, consisted almost entirely of tank engines, largely of 0-6-0T and 0-6-2T types. This wealth of variety inevitably resulted in wholesale scrapping during the early years, and replacement by standard designs of G.W.R. origin; notably the 56xx Class of 0-6-2Ts, already featured in several illustrations. The only tender engines in later years were to be found on the Taff Vale (page 71) and the Barry, which had four of the 0-8-0s illustrated here, These were built by Sharp Stewart in 1887-8 for a railway in Sweden but were never delivered, being eventually taken over by the Barry Railway. They were among the first eight-coupled tender engines to be seen in Britain. No.1390 was photographed at Barry on 1 May 1927; all four were broken up between 1927 and 1930.

194
GREAT WESTERN
200

708
23717
RN
GREAT WESTERN

Penarth shed in May 1927, showing 0-6-0T No.699 (formerly Barry No.1), one of five built in 1888. Scrapped in 1931. In the background is Taff Vale 0-6-2T No.500.

ngines at Cardiff East Dock shed, 1 May 1927; Barry 0-6-0ST No.708 and 0-6-0T No.211, whilst in the ackground is former Cardiff Railway 0-6-2T No.161.

-4-2T No.1316 at Barry, 1 May 1927, one of the last type of Barry engine built for passenger service. There were leven of these built between 1897 and 1899, but none lasted after 1930.

These impressive 0-6-2Ts were the last of a long line of engines of that type built by the Taff Vale. Introduced in 1912, 58 of them had been built by 1921, of which No.376, seen here at Barry, had appeared in 1920. All were eventually rebuilt with Swindon taper boilers, and all lasted into the Nationalisation era, being withdrawn during the 1950s.

G.W.R. No.2181 (formerly Brecon & Merthyr No.5) and No.796 (formerly Taff Vale No.265) in Swindon yard, 11 September 1927, awaiting scrapping.

A Royal occasion on the Taff Vale Railway, June 1912; 4-4-2T No. 173, decorated to haul the Royal train conveying King George V, at Porth. There were six of these engines, built in 1888 and 1891; all were scrapped by the G.W.R. between 1925 and 1927.

Apart from the Barry 0-8-0s already mentioned, the Taff Vale was the only one of the South Wales valley lines to use tender engines in later years — all 0-6-0s, although there had at one time been some ancient 2-4-0s. No. 920 (formerly T.V.R. No. 337), seen here at Penarth in 1927, was one of the last of the 0-6-0s built in 1882. All had gone by the end of 1927. After 1889, construction of tender engines ceased; thereafter nothing but tank engines — principally 0-6-2Ts, which had been introduced in 1885 — were built.

Withdrawal of the older South Wales engines was rapid in the early years of the grouping, and many were to be found in Swindon yard awaiting their fate. A typical view taken on 11 September 1927 shows Barry 0-4-4T No. 4 (B.R. No. 68) in the foreground, whilst next in line are respectively Nos. 100 and 129 (both Rhymney 0-6-2STs), No. 454 (T.V. 0-6-2T) and No. 695 (Cardiff 0-6-0ST).

455

The Port Talbot had also five 0-8-2 tanks, similar to those of the Barry (page 67); all but one of these were scrapped between 1926 and 1935, the survivor remaining just long enough to come into B.R. stock, not being withdrawn until February 1948. Photographed in Danygraig shed, 7 July 1947.

Brecon & Merthyr 0-6-2T No. 1372 (late B. & M. No. 45) built in 1915, at Bassaleg in June 1927, rebuilt with Swindon boiler. It survived to be renumbered 431 by British Railways, and was scrapped in 1953.

Rhymney 0-6-0ST No. 657 (late R.R. No. 56, built in 1902) at Cardiff Docks, 1 May 1927. It was scrapped in 1928.

Cardiff Railway No. 155 (late C.R. No. 35, built in 1908), rebuilt with Swindon boiler, at Cardiff East Dock on 5 May 1951.

Neath & Brecon No.2199 (late N. & B. No.1), built in 1872. This 0-6-0ST was sold out of service in 1931, and later worked at Broomhill Colliery in Northumberland, where this photograph was taken in 1949. It was scrapped about 1955. [F. Jones]

Rhondda & Swansea Bay 0-6-0T No.173 (late R. & S.B. No.13) — built in 1894, and scrapped in 1936. The R. & S.B.R. brought 37 engines into G.W.R. stock at the grouping, mostly 0-6-2Ts, together with some standard Great Western saddle and pannier tanks, which had previously been acquired from the parent company and now returned to the fold. Apart from a couple of these, all other R. & S.B.R. engines had disappeared by 1940. [F. Jones]

In 1903, the Alexandra Docks at Newport had purchased ten engines from the Mersey Railway, which had become redundant owing to electrification. These consisted of three 0-6-4Ts and seven 2-6-2Ts, all of which had gone by 1932. Two additional 2-6-2Ts based on the original design were, however, obtained in 1920, the last new engines for the Alexandra Docks, and one of these, No. 1205, survived into B.R. days. It is seen here at Cardiff (Canton) on 10 September 1951.
[R. M. Casserley]

One of the Mersey 0-6-4Ts already mentioned, No. 22, at Alexandra Docks, 5 August 1905. It was allocated the G.W.R. number 1344 at the grouping but never carried it, being scrapped in 1923.
[K.A.C.R. Nunn per L.C.G.B.]

A number of shunting locomotives were taken over by the G.W.R. at the grouping from two independent concerns responsible for the operation of rail traffic in the extensive docks at Swansea Harbour. One of these, Messrs. Powesland & Mason, had nine engines, all four-coupled saddle tanks. Seen here at Danygraig 7 July 1947 is one of these, built by Hawthorn Leslie in 1903, which became G.W.R. No. 942 (later No. 1153).

No. 943 (later No. 1142) was a former Swansea Harbour Trust engine, built by Hudswell Clarke in 1911, also at Danygraig, 7 July 1947. The Swansea Harbour Trust had fourteen locomotives, three 0-6-0STs and the rest 0-4-0STs.

Llanelli & Mynydd Mawr Railway 0-6-0ST *Hilda,* built by Hudswell Clarke in 1917, became G.W.R. No.359; seen at Danygraig, 8 September 1951, from where it worked until withdrawn in 1954.

Burry Port & Gwendraeth Valley 0-6-0ST No.2196 *Gwendraeth* in Llanelli shed, 9 September 1951.

Danygraig was a mecca for miscellaneous locomotives in early post-war years. This one — a Peckett engine of 1900 — was originally acquired by B.R. in July 1948, after Nationalisation, from Ystalyfera Tinworks; although never a Great Western engine, it was given the number 1 in the Western Region series. Named *Hercules,* it gravitated to Danygraig, where this photograph was taken on 27 August 1948, having taken its place among the other dock engines. It was scrapped in 1954.

A typical view of Danygraig, with a selection of its 'miscellanea' on view on 7 July 1947. Leading the row is G.W.R. 0-4-0T No.1103, one of six built in 1926 for dock work. The others are an early 0-6-0PT, No.1945, together with other dock tanks, and (fifth in line) *Hilda* already portrayed on page 79.

Pontypool Road shed in 1935, showing Nos. 2667 and 2672, two of the outside-framed 2-6-0s, dating back to 1901 and known as the 'Aberdare goods'. They were extensively used in South Wales until their extinction in 1949. [F. Jones]

A freight running through Cardiff station on 28 August 1948 behind 2-8-2T No. 7225. This class was extensively used in South Wales, being ideally suited for short haul workings of heavy coal trains. They had been rebuilt in 1934-6 from 2-8-0Ts of the type illustrated on page 62.

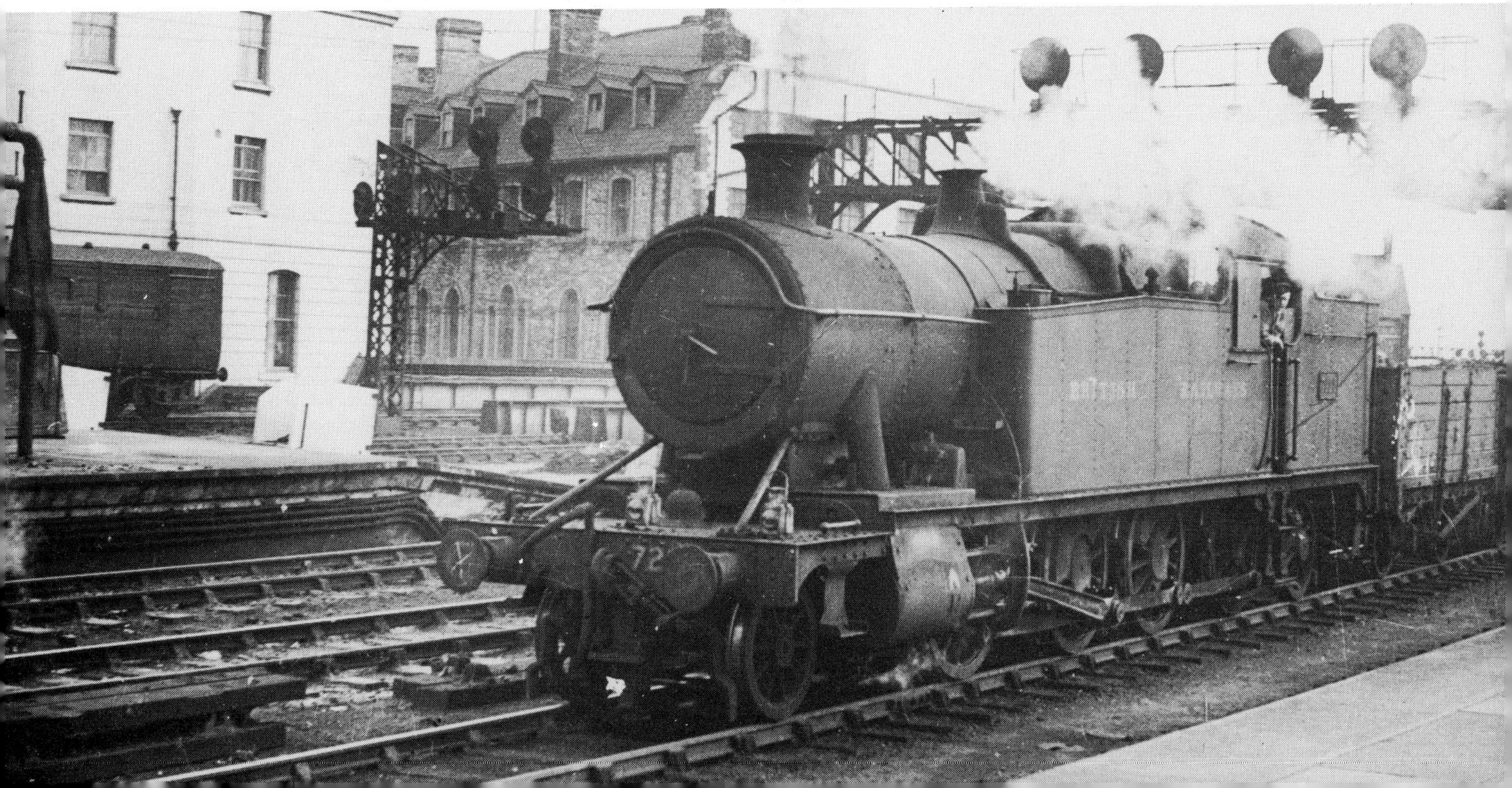

The various major steelworks in South Wales, such as Ebbw Vale, Port Talbot and others, also at one tin employed considerable numbers of steam locomotives. This view, taken at Llanelli Steelworks c 25 September 1965, shows one of those which spent nearly all their time in the confines of the furnaces, rare emerging into daylight. *Christopher* was the most modern of these, having been built by Andrew Barclay in 195 It was scrapped along with the others in 1968, when steam was finally dispensed with at this works.

To present a full picture of industrial railways in South Wales during the heyday of steam would require a volume in itself, and here only a few examples must suffice. The numerous collieries alone could produce many fascinating varieties of steam locomotive, now nearly all replaced by diesels in the relatively few pits still open. One of the most interesting locomotives to be seen in recent years was this old Fox Walker 0-6-0ST, dating from 1874, at Mountain Ash colliery on 10 July 1958. Fortunately, this veteran has found honourable retirement in Bristol Industrial Museum.

There was a large steelworks at Ebbw Vale, the owners of which also operated quarries at Trefil, in the Brecon Mountains, whence they obtained much of their supplies of limestone. This was served by an eight mile-long branch, of particular interest in that it ascended to a height of 1600′ above sea level, the highest summit of any standard gauge railway in the British Isles (thus excluding the Snowdon Mountain Railway) and exceeding the 1498′ of the former Caledonian Railway's Leadhills branch, as well as the 1484′ of the better known Druimuachdar on the Highland. The train seen here at Trefil on 21 June 1959 is in charge of a 1937-built 0-6-0ST.

[T. J. Edgington]

The enormous deposits of slate in North Wales, extending through much of Snowdonia, were amongst the largest in the world, and have been worked for many centuries. This resulted in the creation of extensive railway systems, originally operated by horses, but superseded by steam in the middle of the nineteenth century. The largest of these were the Dinorwic and the Penrhyn — both well-remembered today, as they remained almost entirely operated by steam until their closure in the 1960s, consequent on the rapid decline of the use of slate as a roofing material. This view, taken on 26 August 1954 at Dinorwic, gives but a small idea of the full extent of the quarry, with over twenty

‘levels’, each with its own separate rail system and individual engine shed, interconnected by inclined planes. The engine is one of the numerous Hunslet saddle tanks, *Wild Aster,* many of which have been preserved, not only in Britain but also in America. With about 30 examples having survived, this was until recently the most numerous preserved class of locomotive, but it has now been surpassed by the WD Austerity 0-6-0STs, with some 50 examples of these now in private ownership. Another view at Llanberis, 26 June 1956: *King of the Scarlets* amongst literally a sea of slate. This engine has now found a new home in Canada. [R. M. Casserley]

n the heights of the Penrhyn Quarries at Bethesda, *Pamela,* another Hunslet, is seen shunting on June 1956. This locomotive, built in 1906, is now owned by J. Vernon, of Newbold Vernon, icester.

Penrhyn engines lined up outside a shed on the upper reaches of the quarry system, 25 June 1956. They had to be moved up and down cable-worked inclines at the Dinorwic quarries, and were only returned to the main workshops at 'base camp' when needing heavy repairs. From left to right are:

Cegin	(Barclay, 1931; now in the United States)
Lilian	(Hunslet, 1883; privately preserved at Guildford)
Edward Sholto	(Hunslet, 1909; preserved at Ontario, Canada)
Lilla	(Hunslet, 1891; preserved by J. B. Latham, Woking)
Gertrude	(Hunslet, 1909; now in the Science Museum, Toronto, Canada).

Another view at Bethesda Quarries on the same day, showing *Marchlyn,* built by Avonside in 1933. The locomotive is now in the United States.

Both the Dinorwic and the Penrhyn main lines ran down to the coast, whence the slate could be shipped abroad to destinations all over the world. The Padarn Railway, the seven mile-long line from Llanberis to Dinorwic, was of 4′ gauge, against the 1′ 11″ of the quarry system, and required its own engines, although the wagons themselves were transported on specially adapted vehicles as seen on this train alongside Llanberis Lake, 27 June 1956. Part of the route has now been converted into a pleasure line; amongst other locomotives on it are some former Dinorwic quarry engines, including *Wild Aster,* featured on page 84.

A train en route to Port Penrhyn, on the main line of the Penrhyn Railway, 11 August 1953. The viaduct carries the L.M.S. main line of the old Chester & Holyhead Railway, between Aber and Bangor.

Port Dinorwic quayside at the lower end of the Padarn Railway, served by a standard gauge branch off the L.M.S.R. In the interchange sidings is ex-L. & Y.R. 0-6-0 No.52230, together with Dinorwic narrow gauge 0-4-0WT No.70; 25 April 1954.

Blanche, one of the three Penrhyn 'main line' locomotives, at Port Penrhyn. The latter is also connected to the main B.R. system by a standard gauge branch. This locomotive is now better known, together with its sister *Linda,* on the Festiniog Railway, rebuilt as a 2-4-0ST with tender (page 91). The third engine, *Charles,* survives in Penrhyn Castle Museum.

The group of narrow gauge railways in North Wales, now collectively known for publicity purposes as the 'Great Little Trains of Wales', are so well known that any detailed account of them here would be superfluous. It is sufficient to recall that the 2′ 3″ gauge Tal-y-Llyn was the pioneer of the movement, which has now spread not only throughout Great Britain but to many foreign parts as well. The Tal-y-Llyn, threatened with closure in 1950, through the efforts of a group of enthusiasts in the Midlands, became the first privately preserved railway in the world. This view, taken at Towyn on 1 June 1932, when it was still maintaining a precarious independent existence, shows No.2 *Dolgoch,* one of only two engines the railway had possessed since its opening in 1864.

The story of the neighbouring Ffestiniog, which followed the example of the Tal-y-Llyn, is somewhat similar, except that in this case the railway had lain derelict for several years and had to be completely renovated, whereas the Tal-y-Llyn is able to boast that it 'never closed'. The Ffestiniog could not be opened throughout, owing to part of the line having been submerged by the construction of a reservoir, but a diversion is under construction, and it will shortly be reopened again through to Blaenau Ffestiniog. Some of the original Ffestiniog engines are still at work, including two of the famous 'Fairlie' double-enders, but this view, taken on 30 May 1966, shows one of the later acquisitions, *Linda* (see page 89), rounding Horse Shoe Curve south of Tan-y-Bwlch. *Linda* has here acquired a tender, but since then, like her sister *Blanche* has now been fitted with leading pony trucks, making them 2-4-0STs with tender; they are now also oil fired. [M. Mensing]

8

THE EARL
822
71702

The term 'Heyday of Steam' still well and truly applies to the Snowdon Mountain, Britain's only rack railway, for since its opening in 1896 it has never employed any other motive power. Four out of the original five engines built in 1895-6, together with three later ones of 1922-3, are still busily engaged during the summer season. This view, taken on 29 August 1965, shows one of the earlier ones, No.2 *Enid,* between Clogwyn and the Summit, together with two other trains, at the passing place at Clogwyn in the background. In the distance can be seen some of the galleries of Dinorwic slate quarries. [M. Mensing]

e Vale of Rheidol, running from Aberystwyth to Devil's Bridge, became part of the G.W.R. at the grouping, d eventually of British Railways. It has the distinction of being the only B.R. line still steam-worked, open ring the summer season. This view, taken on 26 August 1948, shows the old terminus at Aberystwyth, with ins ready to depart. There are three of these little 1′ 11½″ gauge 2-6-2Ts retained for working the line, of which o, No.8 on the left and No.1213 (since renumbered No.9) are seen here.

e 2′ 6″ gauge Welshpool & Llanfair was an offshoot of the Cambrian, and as such was taken over by the G.W.R. the grouping in 1923. Passenger services ceased in 1931 and goods in 1956, when a preservation society was ugurated. This has been able to re-open most of the line, except the eastern part running through the streets of elshpool. Seen here is one of the two engines, G.W.R. No.822 *The Earl,* on 24 August 1948. This locomotive, w again No.1 (together with No.2 *Countess,* which was also fortunately saved at the time of closure) now works e restored railway, together with some new additions.

The yearly Tal-y-Llyn Special from London to Towyn for the Annual General Meeting provided opportunit for the utilisation of unusual motive power between Shrewsbury and Towyn, of which full advantage was take In 1955 ex-L.S.W.R. T9 4-4-0 No.30304, assisted by a 'Dukedog', was provided, and in 1956 another Southe engine, one of Wainwright's handsome D Class 4-4-0s, appeared — the only instances one can recall of t penetration of S.R. engines into the Principality, apart from some through workings to Cardiff from Portsmou during the 1930s. No.31075 is here seen piloting a Dean goods, at the halt for water at Welshpo 22 September 1956. The Southern 4-4-0 was manned by enginemen from Reading South on a lodging turn. It w withdrawn from service two months later, the last of the class to remain in traffic; fortunately No.737 is preserv in York Museum.
[P. B. Whitehou

The annual Towyn Special leaving Moat Lane on 28 September 1937; another stranger to the countr ex-L. & Y.R. 2-4-2T No.50781 is piloting 'Dukedog' No.9031.
[R. J. Buckle

As far as steam railtours over main lines are concerned, now happily with us once again after several years complete ban, undoubtedly their heyday was the period of the late 1950s and early 1960s, when it was possible to organise tours over unusual routes and, moreover, with interesting engines — often older ones dating back to pre-grouping days. One of these was a Stephenson Locomotive Society Special on 5 January 1958 over the L.N.W.R. Abergavenny-Merthyr line, since entirely closed. Opportunity was taken to utilise the last active Webb 0-6-2T (No.58926; now preserved) together with an ex-L.N.W.R. 0-8-0 (No.49121), both of them types which had been regularly in use over this hilly route. The train pauses here at Brynmawr for the engines to take water.
[R. J. Buckley]

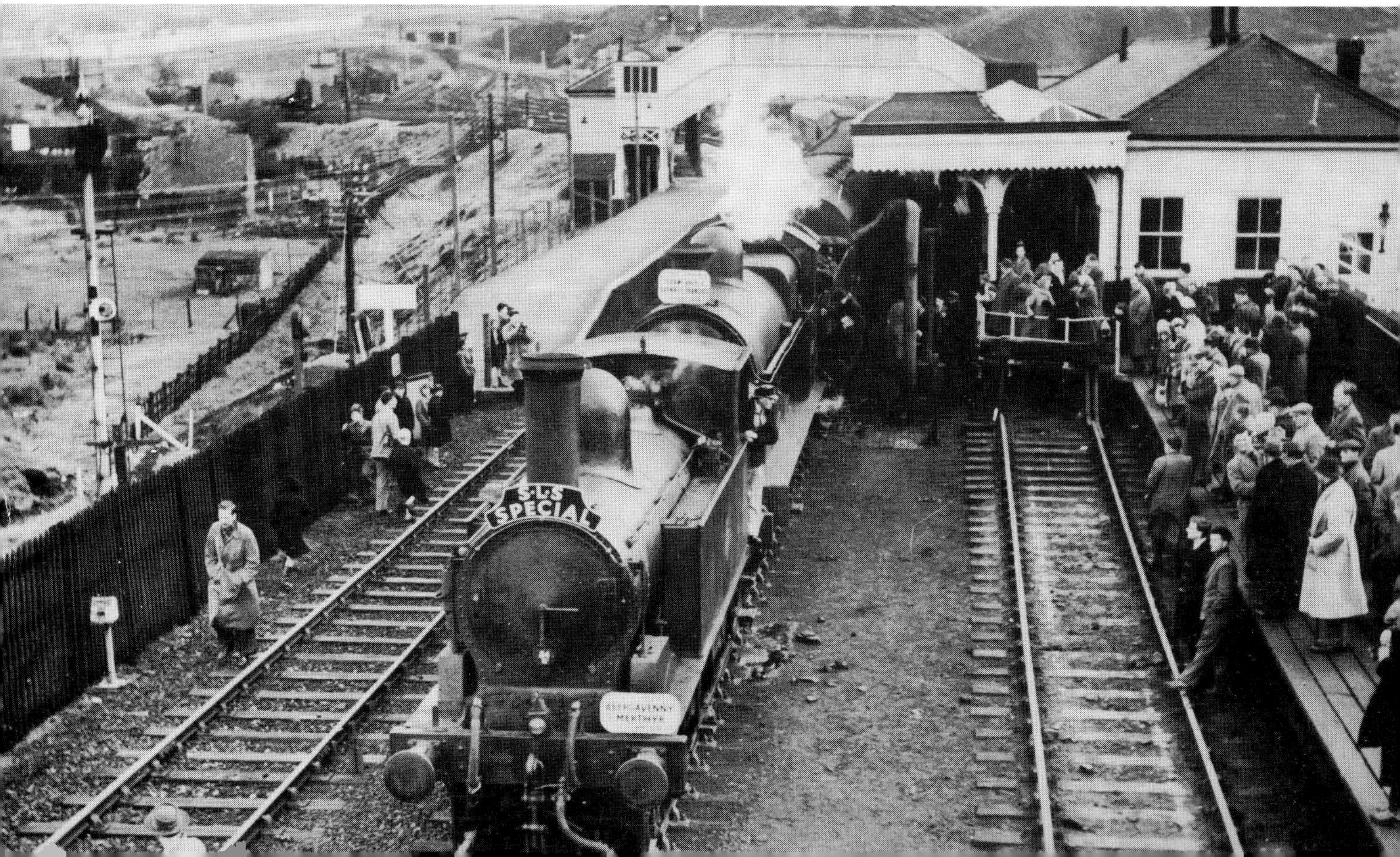

WELSHPOOL
JUNCTION FOR
SHREWSBURY, STAFFORD,
BIRMINGHAM, LONDON
31075

TALYLLYN
RAILWAY
SPECIAL
50781

The last steam train to run to Fishguard was a special organised by the Stephenson Locomotive Society and the Railway Correspondence & Travel Society, and is seen here pausing at St. Clears on 26 September 1965, in charge of 'Grange' Class No.6859 *Yiewsley Grange*.

MIDLAND
NORTH EASTERN
STEAM
GREAT WESTERN
STEAM MISCELLANY
BODMIN AND WADEBRIDGE
BR STANDARD STEAM
IN ACTION
NARROW GAUGE
STEAM
A PICTORIAL SURVEY
GREAT WESTERN
BRANCH LINE STEAM
DIESELS
ON SCOTTISH REGION
BR DIESELS
IN ACTION
H. C. CASSERLEY
IRISH RAILWAYS
in the heyday of steam
SOUTHERN
188
THE LYNTON & BARNSTAPLE RAILWAY
THE WARSHIPS
42/43 DIESEL - HYDRAULICS
STEAM
LONDON MIDLAND
STEAM IN ACTION 4
NORTH EASTERN
STEAM
IN ACTION
8F
2-8-0
STEAM